T0193161

HIS PERFECT WAY
The Hermit Crab Story

Written and Illustrated by

VIVIAN COATS

authorHOUSE®

AuthorHouse™
1663 Liberty Drive
Bloomington, IN 47403
www.authorhouse.com
Phone: 1-800-839-8640

First published by AuthorHouse 3/14/2011

ISBN: 978-1-4567-3482-4 (sc)

Library of Congress Control Number: 2011901722

Printed in the United States of America
Bloomington, Indiana

This book is printed on acid-free paper.

Scripture taken from the HOLY BIBLE,
NEW INTERNATIONAL VERSION
Copyright 1973, 1978, 1984 International Bible Society.
Used by permission of Zondervan Bible Publishers.

ACKNOWLEDGEMENTS

*The author gratefully acknowledges the loved ones that believed
and worked so diligently for this book ministry.*

Jim Coats my beloved husband who continues to say, "You Can!", and I do!

*Jamie Aylstock our daughter and co-editor. Jamie and her husband Jason
continue to prayerfully and financially encourage this book ministry.*

*My sister Diane Arthurton who has given generously
of her time to edit untold pages of my books.*

*Fred and Linda Aylstock who spend their time updating my website,
along with praying and giving words of encouragement.*

*Our pastors Susan and Jerry Williams who are not afraid to preach the word of
God in truth. They continue to pray for God's direction for this book ministry.*

*Roger and Sheila Bouchard missionaries to America who gave
the first financial assistance to see these books printed.*

*Trinity Church/Rainbow of Love School continues to
pray and support this important book ministry.*

*There are a multitude of people that continue to purchase these books,
pray for this book ministry and give me words of encouragement-
you know who you are! A generous thank you to all! Miracles
and Interventions really do happen every single day!*

*Joyfully yours,
Vivian Coats*

Other Books by Vivian Coats

In His Love

Safe In His Love

His Special Love

His Star

His Perfect Way

The Hermit Crab Story is Written Just for You!

The ocean has a deadly rip current. When a swimmer fights against this flow, he/she will drown. The only way to get out of this deadly current is to relax and let it carry you. When we go with God's flow for our lives, we will be successful. Hermit Crab goes with the flow and safely makes it to land.

Many of us ask God to be the Lord of all. But then we are selective concerning what pieces of our lives we will give to Him. He wants you to begin each day with a good morning to Him. At the noon hour, take a moment to remember your help always comes from God. Seek His perfect way for the rest of your day. And every night, he wants your sleep to be sweet in Him.

Starting today, give God all the pieces of your life. He will counsel you, watch over you, and show you His perfect way!

Joyfully and Safely In His Special Love,

Vivian Coats

Hermit Crab fun facts:

Some experts believe Hermit Crabs are not closely related to true crabs.

These eggs are brick red in the first stage. The eggs will turn dark grey when they are ready to hatch. The female will fling her eggs out to sea, and they will burst on contact with the saltwater. There will be 4-6 more cycles taking place in the salty water and lasting about 40-60 days. Near the end of the final stages, it will metamorphosis into a megalopa, which looks like a lobster/hermit crab. This lobster/hermit crab stage will last about a month. At this time, the hermit crab's gills are adapting to breathe air. They are spending longer periods out of the water. Eventually, the megalopa buries itself to molt and then resurfaces as a young hermit crab. Now if it was placed indefinitely under water, it would drown.

They are found all over the world.

There are about 800 known species.

They have so many battles to be won. They are constantly fighting against climate, predators, and even other hermit crabs!

They can live for 15-40 years, but most only live 6-12 months.

Throughout the years, they continue to grow and are always in need of a new shell. They use their antennas to feel out new homes. Some will even live under pieces of coconut.

They come in a variety of colors.

They love to hide in the cleft of the rock.

As Christians, that is the perfect place to be because Jesus is our Rock.

Hermit Crab was born in the ocean.

He was just a little egg.

So God created the great creatures of the sea and every living and moving thing with which the water teems. And God saw that it was good.

Genesis 1:21a,b,c,e (NIV)

One day, Hermit Crab began to walk. He had grown ten legs. He had six legs for walking and four more were growing in the back.

I praise you because I am fearfully and wonderfully made;
your works are wonderful, I know that full well.

Psalm 139:14 (NIV)

Hermit Crab knew he must put his hope in the Lord. It was time to let the ocean's current take him to land.

There is the sea, vast and spacious, teeming with creatures beyond number-living things both large and small. Psalm 104:25 (NIV)

Hermit Crab needed to find a
home for his soft body.

Crabs love to shop for new homes.

He tried on all the things he
found on the beach.

In his heart a man plans his course, but the Lord determines his steps.

Proverbs 16:9 (NIV)

The can was too high.

He guides the humble in what is right and teaches them his way. All the ways of the Lord are loving and faithful for those who keep the demands of his covenant.

Psalm 25:9&10 (NIV)

The towel was too long.

I will instruct you and teach you in the way you should go; Psalm 32:8a (NIV)

The boat was too big.

I will counsel you and watch over you. Psalm 32:8b(NIV)

The bucket was too wide.

Show me your ways, O Lord, teach me your paths; Psalm 25:4 (NIV)

Hermit Crab was getting hotter. He would be in danger if he became dry! His legs were hurting, and he was tired.

But those who hope in the Lord will renew their strength. They will run and not grow weary, they will walk and not be faint. Isaiah 40:31a,c,d (NIV)

Hermit Crab began to pray. He knew
God's way was perfect. He asked God
to show him the perfect house.

*" For I know the plans I have for you," declares the Lord, " plans to prosper
you and not to harm you, plans to give you hope and a future. Then you
will call upon me and come and pray to me, and I will listen to you. You
will seek me and find me when you seek me with all your heart. I will be
found by you," declares the Lord. Jeremiah 29:11,12,13,14a (NIV)*

Then Hermit Crab saw a sea shell wash up on the sand.

It is God who arms me with strength and makes my way perfect.

Psalm 18:32 (NIV)

24

The shell was just his size.
It was a perfect fit!

As for God, his way is perfect; the word of the Lord is flawless. He is a shield for all who take refuge in him. Psalm 18:30 (NIV)

Now Hermit Crab with his new home would be safe in the cracks of the rocks.

The Lord is my rock, my fortress and my deliverer; my God is my rock, in whom I take refuge. Psalm 18:2a,b (NIV)

Hermit Crab fell asleep giving thanks
to God for giving him a perfect
day in His perfect way.

*I will lie down and sleep in peace, for you alone, O Lord,
make me dwell in safety. Psalm 4:8 (NIV)*

Printed in the United States
by Baker & Taylor Publisher Services